M000187754

Guided Journal

A LITTLE BIT OF

CHAKRAS

THIS BOOK BELONGS TO

_____

_____

_____

Guided Journal

A LITTLE BIT OF
CHAKRAS

YOUR PERSONAL PATH
TO ENERGY HEALING

AMY LEIGH & CHAD MERCREE

STERLING ETHOS
New York

DEDICATION

WE DEDICATE THIS BOOK TO OUR AGENT, Lisa Hagan, one of the kindest, smartest women we know. She has brought so much consciousness-raising, wellness-enhancing media into the world and done it with tremendous grace and thoughtfulness.

STERLING ETHOS
New York

An Imprint of Sterling Publishing Co., Inc.
1166 Avenue of the Americas
New York, NY 10036

Portions of this publication previously published as *A Little Bit of Chakras.*

ISBN 978-1-4549-4032-6

Distributed in Canada by Sterling Publishing Co., Inc.
c/o Canadian Manda Group, 664 Annette Street
Toronto, Ontario M6S 2C8, Canada
Distributed in the United Kingdom by GMC Distribution Services
Castle Place, 166 High Street, Lewes, East Sussex BN7 1XU, England
Distributed in Australia by NewSouth Books
University of New South Wales, Sydney, NSW 2052, Australia

For information about custom editions, special sales, and premium and corporate purchases,
please contact Sterling Special Sales at 800-805-5489 or specialsales@sterlingpublishing.com.

Manufactured in Singapore

2 4 6 8 10 9 7 5 3 1

sterlingpublishing.com

Cover design by Elizabeth Mihaltse Lindy
Interior design by Sharon Jacobs

Image Credits:
Fuzzimo.com: cover; Getty Images/iStock: transiastock: throughout;
Shutterstock: satit_srihin: cover, throughout; Transia Design: cover, throughout

❈ CONTENTS ❦

Crown Chakra

 Third Eye Chakra

 Throat Chakra

 Heart Chakra

 Solar Plexus Chakra

 Sacral Chakra

 Root Chakra

INTRODUCTION: WHAT ARE CHAKRAS?

A Little Bit of Chakras Guided Journal introduces you to the mystical world of chakras, wheels of spinning energy located in specific areas of the body. Chakras are concentrations of vital life force within the body formed when lines of energy running through the body overlap and cross. For thousands of years, mystics have worked with and studied chakras and incorporated them into a wide variety of spiritual practices.

Working with chakra energy in a positive way has been linked to increased lifespan; physical, mental, and emotional health; and overall personal well-being.

Conflicting information on the number, location, and purpose of chakras makes any comprehensive guide difficult to compile. This book focuses on the Western view of chakras found in contemporary New Age literature, as opposed to traditional Eastern mystical views. Therefore, we focus on seven primary chakras, running from the base of the spine to the top of the head.

Each chakra is linked to organs within the body, emotional and mental attitudes, physical health or disease, colors, sounds, psychic abilities, and many other things. Some of these associations are symbolic, others based on mathematical formulas, and some on personal opinion by well-regarded spiritual practitioners. There is a widely held belief in the New Age movement that energy and consciousness are the same thing, and in this sense, chakra energy also holds aspects of our consciousness. Yogis and mystics have found many ways of working with these centers of consciousness, and we'll share some exercises and meditations to help you connect on a personal level with at least seven of your chakras.

Chakras are a part of a much larger human auric field. The aura is a dynamic field of energy that surrounds and permeates the human body. It is in constant motion like a pulsating cloud, and its quality, color, and vibrations change from moment to moment, thought to thought, feeling to feeling. Psychics believe we spiritually connect to other people, the world around us, and to the entire universe through our energy body, the aura. The physical body is simply the densest aspect of our earthly being. The aura more truly represents who we really are and the chakras are an important part of our auras because they connect our dense physical and our lighter auric fields together.

Chakras are concentrated points of energy within us, and when they are healthy, vital life energy flows through them unimpeded. When this happens, their colors are bright and clear. The opposite occurs during energetic imbalances; their colors are more dense, dark, and dull. Oftentimes when psychics "read" people they are tuning in to the quality of energy they detect within our auric fields, including our chakras. Just as medical doctors believe we store memories physically in our brains, though the exact mechanism has yet to be discovered, so psychics believe we store memories spiritually in our auric field. Psychics can "see" memories, emotional states, and past lives—really all kinds of information in our auric fields and chakras.

The concept of chakras has been around for over two thousand years in India, and for thousands of years Chinese Taoists moved their chi, or vital life force, through various "stations" that correspond more or less to the concept of Indian chakras. Both systems used visualization to bring human awareness to these points of energy found within the body, typically during periods of meditation. Thanks to written records, we're able to see the discovery and changing perceptions about chakras and the larger energy field surrounding humans, the aura, through thousands of years of human history.

Between the dawn of Indian Upanishad philosophy and Chinese Taoist philosophy and the New Age movement of today, the concept of chakras has drastically changed. Different religions, sects within religions, philosophers, and mystics around the world described chakras differently, and there is no one consensus about what they look like or even where they're located. However, over time, ideas about chakras have brought them from an abstract visualization to a living, breathing, integral part of human consciousness. This book shares contemporary Western views about chakras being energy centers that influence physical, emotional, and spiritual healing and well-being.

A Little Bit of Chakras Guided Journal is laid out sequentially from one chakra to the next, moving up the body from the base of the spine to the top of the head. We recognize seven main chakras in the body, though many "minor" chakras are also recognized. A chapter is devoted to each of the seven chakras—root, sacral, solar plexus, heart, throat, third eye, and crown. Each chakra is associated with certain colors, organs, emotional and physical states, elements, sounds, and other things. Some people see chakras as key concepts in attaining advanced levels of spiritual development, for example, in some types of kundalini yoga. Once you learn to work with the energies of each chakra, it's possible to incorporate working with them into any spiritual practice.

Thanks to the mini-New Age movement of the late 1800s and early 1900s, spiritual concepts from the East have been trickling into the West for over one hundred years. People from all walks of life and all spiritual faiths have incorporated Eastern philosophies into their lives.

We hope you enjoy *A Little Bit of Chakras Guided Journal.* The world of chakras has a colorful past that has contributed greatly to the spiritual, physical, emotional, and mental well-being of thousands upon thousands of spiritual seekers. We wish the same for you.

THIS JOURNAL

Join us for an interactive journey through your chakras! In this journal, you can glean the basics of how your chakras work and delve into them through the transformative power of writing. The journal can be used on its own, or in conjunction with *A Little Bit of Chakras,* which includes more in-depth information on some of the material in this journal.

What areas of your life and body would you like to optimize?
Write about them below in an easy numbered list. Then, you can refer
to this journal and determine which chakras are best to optimize to
accomplish those goals. Sometimes, just bringing our attention to an
area of life or the body can effortlessly open the door to healing and
inspiration. Allow that now as you journal below!

MULADHARA— THE ROOT CHAKRA

IN SANSKRIT, THE WORD MULADHARA MEANS "ROOT support." The root chakra is located at the base of the spine. Most traditions describe it as red in color. Some people see the shades of red as bright cherry and some as more on the maroon end of the spectrum. Part of the color perception of a chakra involves how bright and light it is—the lighter and brighter, the better. Since chakras are made of energy we want it to be clear and luminous, not muddy or dim.

In Tantric tradition, it has four deep red petals.

Muladhara governs survival, security, and your walk in the world. This chakra is all about support. It supports the rest of your physical body because it is at the base of the spine. It relates to how supported you feel in this world materially. A healthy and clear root chakra will bring vitality to your feet and legs. The energy flowing there will be strong and rich.

When in balance, muladhara resonates security, stillness, and stability. It helps you feel safe in the world and sure that your needs will be met, especially your basic physical needs for shelter, food, water, sleep, clothing, and material comfort. Because of our urge to be stable and secure in this world, we all seek strength in the root chakra.

Gravity is this chakra's most influential force. In essence, it holds your feet to the ground gently and effortlessly. Being "grounded" is a term you may have heard that refers to the root chakra. Being grounded means that you are rooted and present in your body and on the planet.

The body and presence are critical to health and happiness. Ideally, the body feels grounded and present. This feeling stems from the security of the root chakra. Strength and balance in the root chakra paves the way for a life that is stable and secure.

How rooted to the earth do you feel right now?

How present do you feel in your body?

_____

_____

_____

_____

_____

_____

_____

_____

_____

_____

_____

_____

_____

_____

_____

_____

_____

_____

_____

_____

_____

Bring your attention to your first chakra and jot down three adjectives to describe how it feels now. Why did you choose these three words?

_____

_____

_____

_____

_____

_____

_____

_____

_____

_____

_____

_____

_____

_____

_____

_____

_____

_____

_____

Next, journal three words to describe how you would like it to feel.

1. _____

2. _____

3. _____

_____

Reflect on the three words you chose in the space below.

_____

_____

_____

_____

_____

_____

_____

_____

_____

_____

_____

_____

_____

_____

_____

_____

Now, make a list of three things you can do (like taking a walk in nature) that could help bring your first chakra into the state you desire.

1. _____

_____

_____

_____

_____

_____

2. _____

_____

_____

_____

_____

_____

3. _____

_____

_____

_____

_____

Now, go do one or more! Journal about how this felt in your body.

What did you notice?

_____

_____

_____

_____

_____

_____

_____

_____

_____

_____

_____

_____

_____

_____

_____

_____

_____

_____

_____

_____

SVADHISHTHANA—
THE SACRAL
CHAKRA

IN SANSKRIT, THE WORD *SVADHISHTHANA* MEANS "sweetness." The sacral chakra is located in the lower abdomen and womb. It is generally thought to be orange. Some people picture it as a clear, vivid orange, like the color of the fruit. Some picture it a bit lighter or more golden. The brighter you perceive the chakra to be, the healthier it is. We want your chakras to be luminous, clear, and full of light. This means the energy is flowing and balanced. To unblock energy in your chakras, you focus on filling them with light and letting go of any past density that you may hold there.

Tantric traditions believe that this chakra has six vermilion red petals. In this chapter, we will be working from the Western theory of chakras, where the chakra is orange.

Svadhishthana governs pleasure, desire, sexuality, sensuality, and procreation. It is all about the sweetness of life and feeling good.

This chakra enlivens your world experience by engaging your senses and emotions. This is a complicated, rich, and, when in balance, rewarding chakra. A healthy and vibrant sacral chakra will help you enjoy life to the fullest. It brings vitality through pleasure and enjoyment and can be a source of great joy.

When in balance, svadhishthana gives you the ability to navigate change and the polarities of life. It also resonates pleasure, movement, emotions, sexuality, and nurturance. It helps you engage in the sensory experience of living and integrate that energy into your subtle bodies. The human urge to procreate and be close to a romantic partner is part of the dance of the sacral chakra.

Attraction of opposites is the chief force influencing svadhishthana. You can think of this as the attraction of opposites from a purely physiological sense with men and women and how the areas of the body governed by the sacral chakra are opposite in a way that can result in procreation. That is why this chakra is your creative energy center. It is where you birth what you want to manifest or share with the world.

Feeling lively and creative is critical to a happy life. Ideally, you feel vital, alive, creative, and you experience the sensory pleasures of life (not just sexual) daily. Those feelings stem from a healthy sacral chakra. Creativity and sweetness in the sacral chakra pave the way for a life of enjoyment and feeling good.

Your sacral chakra is associated with your ovaries or testicles. These endocrine glands are the ones that most govern this chakra. Endocrine glands produce hormones. The ovaries produce eggs to be fertilized and they also produce estrogen, progesterone, and testosterone. The testicles produce sperm and testosterone.

If these endocrine glands do not function correctly, impotence, low libido, and infertility can result. In modern life, we are exposed to myriad chemicals and xenoestrogens (fake estrogens). Xenoestrogens are substances that fool the body into thinking they are estrogen. Main sources of xenoestrogens are traditional household cleaning products like bleach, dry-cleaning chemicals, and plastics. Eliminating or reducing your exposure to these substances may help your body. Mind-body remedies for supporting these endocrine glands include guided visualization and acupuncture.

Other parts of the body associated with the sacral chakra are the uterus, genitals, kidneys, bladder, circulatory system, prostate, and sacral nerve plexus. Some potential signs of sacral chakra dysfunction include uterine, bladder, and prostate trouble; kidney illness; stiff lower back; and anemia.

Emotional, mental, and spiritual dysfunction of this chakra includes sex addiction, out of control emotions, or lack of emotion responsiveness.

To encourage health and vitality in this chakra, you can view clear, bright shades of orange, especially if you feel the chakra is underactive. You can also wear this color. You can wear a softer, more peachy orange to encourage the acceptance of life's sweetness. Since this chakra is specifically associated with life's simple pleasures, you can also engage in any activity that feels healthfully pleasurable for you.

On average about how many times per day do you experience pleasure?

Including sensory and emotional pleasure?

_____

_____

_____

_____

_____

_____

_____

_____

_____

_____

_____

_____

_____

_____

_____

_____

_____

_____

_____

_____

List some existing pleasures in your life below.

1. _____

_____

2. _____

_____

3. _____

_____

4. _____

_____

5. _____

_____

6. _____

_____

7. _____

_____

8. _____

_____

9. _____

_____

10. _____

_____

11.

12.

13.

14.

15.

16.

17.

18.

Next, make a lengthy list of other pleasurable ideas that might appeal to you (things like: eating shaved ice dessert in the bright sun, feeling a light breeze on your skin as you walk on a forest trail, witnessing the light of the full moon limning a meadow of tall grass, cozying up in a plush chenille throw in front of the fireplace).

Afterwards, rewrite this list below. List your favorite one first and so on. Note any conditions that need to be right to enact the activity, like a sunny day or a clear night sky. Now, make a commitment to do one or more per day. You are worth the effort!

1. _____

2. _____

3. _____

4. _____

5. _____

6. _____

7. _____

8. _____

9. _____

10. _____

11. _____

12. _____

13. _____

14. _____

15. _____

16. _____

17. _____

18. _____

19. _____

20. _____

21. _____

22. _____

23. _____

24. _____

25. _____

You can also use this space to free write about your sacral chakra and how you feel about it and how you would like to feel about it.

_____

_____

_____

_____

_____

_____

_____

_____

_____

_____

_____

MANIPURA—THE SOLAR PLEXUS CHAKRA

I N SANSKRIT THE WORD *MANIPURA* MEANS "LUSTROUS gem." Manipura is a chakra located in your solar plexus—the area above your belly button and below your xiphoid process. Most traditions describe this chakra as yellow. Usually it is deemed to be a bright shade, full of vigor. One way that this chakra is judged to be healthy is if it is vibrantly colored and luminous. A great way to imagine the solar plexus chakra is as a brilliant yellow dynamo.

In Tantric traditions, the chakra is believed to be made of ten blue petals and a downward triangle with Hindu solar crosses, and a running ram at the base. In this book, we will focus on the Western model of thinking, which believes this chakra to be yellow.

Manipura governs your personal power, confidence, assertiveness, and will. This chakra is all about power. It empowers the rest of your body, and it relates to your right use of power and will.

The solar plexus chakra creates your uniqueness and enables you to transform through your will and personal power. A bright and clear solar plexus chakra helps you wield your overall personal power in the world.

When in balance, this chakra emanates autonomy, self-esteem, confidence, and free will. It helps you be self-assured and independent in the world. It is meant to facilitate your meeting your own needs for validation and freedom. All people desire to feel sovereign and catalyzing to their own world. Because of these needs, it is a natural human urge to strengthen the solar plexus chakra.

Combustion is the solar plexus chakra's most influential force. It is the essence of transformation and power. It is the flame of metamorphosis. This chakra supplies your vim and vigor. It powers you up and fuels your action in the world. It's essential to accomplishing things that need a lot of dynamic energy.

Your personal power is intrinsically important in your life. Ideally, your body will feel powerful and capable and your sense of self will be strong and healthy. This feeling stems from the energy of your solar plexus chakra. Power and balance in this chakra pave the way for a life of success and results.

The solar plexus chakra is associated with your pancreas. This organ is an exocrine and endocrine gland. We will discuss its exocrine functions in a moment. As an endocrine gland, it secretes the hormones insulin and glucagon to control blood sugar levels.

Dysfunctions of this endocrine gland include hypoglycemia and type 1 diabetes. Hypoglycemia has many causes; one of the rarest is when the pancreas produces too much insulin. With type 1 diabetes, it does not produce enough. Mind-body remedies to help with both of these include tai chi, yoga, and Ayurveda (a Hindu system of medicine that is based on the idea of balance in all bodily systems and proper diet, herbal treatments, and yogic breathing).

Other parts of the body associated with this chakra are the overall digestive system and muscles as well as the exocrine functions of the pancreas, which excretes enzymes to break down proteins, lipids, carbohydrates, and nucleic acids in food. Some body-based chakra dysfunction include ulcers and digestive disorders.

Emotional, spiritual, and mental dysfunction of this chakra are often in the form of excess anger and rage, whether repressed or inappropriately expressed. Typically, people with a "short fuse" need to balance and soothe their solar plexus chakra. Anger management skills can be learned from a qualified professional.

Health and wellness of this chakra can be increased by visually taking in shades of clear yellow. If the chakra is overactive and too much rage and anger are present, then clear pastel yellow can soothe the energy center and help it relax. If the chakra is underactive and you need more confidence to magnify your charm or personal power, then shades of bright, clear, strong, vibrant yellow will be helpful.

To increase the health of the solar plexus chakra, vigorous exercise can be helpful. So can strength training of all kinds. Building your stamina, endurance, and strength all help this chakra function with clarity and ease. Another major way to bolster this chakra is to put extra emphasis on building your self-esteem. Quick ways to do this are: become aware of your inner critic and try to replace those thoughts with positive ones, and create a list of at least thirty wonderful things about yourself. Treat yourself with kindness and respect, and your solar plexus chakra will have an opportunity to clear and strengthen.

Since your will is centered in your solar plexus chakra, it is a very important energy center to have in healthy balance because it affects your ability to push your creations out into the world and move them forward. Your third chakra is a big part of your success in the world. In our society, will energy moves situations in the direction you desire. This has an effect on your career among other things in your life.

You can use your will to move things forward as long as you balance that will by always insuring and intending that everything that transpires is for the highest good of all life, including you. Look for win/win situations in response to circumstances in your life and then know that your will can be strong and individuated, and allow it to flow in the direction you want. It is just like a river of vibration and you can create and step into the infinite, dazzling flow and harness the power of your will to create your best life.

How empowered do you feel in your life? Who is the leader of your life? Write about that below with no judgement, just honesty.

If you had to rate how empowered you feel in the creation of your life circumstances on a scale of 0-100 with 0 being not empowered at all and 100 being completely and totally empowered, what number comes to mind? Expand upon this rating. How does this show up in your life?

A sense of empowerment is crucial to creating the life you desire. Next, make a list of five ways you can claim more dominion and ownership of your life.

1. _____

_____

_____

_____

_____

_____

_____

_____

_____

_____

_____

_____

_____

_____

_____

_____

_____

_____

_____

2.

3.

4.

5.

Now, journal seriously and honestly about how willing you are to take the reins and responsibility for your life. It takes courage. Fear can prevent us from owning our lives completely. Everything you desire may be on the other side of fear. Reflect on these ideas below.

_____

_____

_____

_____

_____

_____

_____

_____

_____

_____

_____

_____

_____

_____

_____

_____

_____

_____

_____

4

ANAHATA— THE HEART CHAKRA

THE SANSKRIT TRANSLATION OF THE WORD *anahata* is "unstruck"—meaning a sound that is made without any two things striking. The heart chakra is located in the center of the chest. Western traditions describe it as green in color. It is generally thought to be bright emerald green. The brighter and more full of light the color is, the healthier the chakra.

In Tantric traditions, it is believed to have twelve deep red petals surrounding a six-pointed star. For the rest of this chapter, we will be focusing on the Western ideas pertaining to this chakra.

Anahata rules love, breath, balance, relationships, and unity. This chakra is all about the higher energies of love and compassion when in balance. It governs matters of romance and friendship and heart connection. When your heart chakra's needs are met, you feel loved, cared for, and you love yourself. The universal urge that we all have to love and be loved originates in the heart chakra.

This chakra's most influential force is equilibrium, which means a state of balance and calmness. This is a type of emotional stability and symmetry. Having a calm and content heart is the essence of the balanced heart chakra's equilibrium.

Love and a happy heart are crucial to your quality of life. Life is about connection and caring, and without it, you may feel bereft and alone. A healthy heart chakra lets you know that you are never alone. You can extend caring to others and yourself and allow your heart to be open and full.

The heart chakra is associated with your thymus gland. Your thymus is most active before puberty. It's seated between your lungs, behind your sternum. Before puberty, your thymus produces lots of thymosin, a hormone that helps your body produce T-cells, which play a vital role in immunity for your whole lifetime.

Endocrine dysfunction associated with the thymus gland can involve lowered immunity. Since most of the thymus's influence happens in childhood, the best way to strengthen the body as an adult is to boost immunity in myriad ways. Two mind-body remedies that can help are meditation and qigong to reduce the effects of stress on your body. General exercise also helps boost immunity, and dry skin brushing may also help.

The other parts of the body associated with the heart chakra are the heart, lungs, hands, and arms. Some potential signs of heart chakra imbalance are heart disease and asthma. Emotional dysfunction of the chakra can include fear of not being loved enough and not being able to fully receive love from others.

To promote health in your heart chakra, you simply must immerse yourself in love in a balanced and healthy way. A great way to give and receive unconditional love is with pets. If you have a pet, you likely already know what this feels like. If you don't, you might want to spend time with a friend's pet and offer it your love and caring. Spending time with kids in your family, especially those who are in early or middle childhood, is another great way to share feelings of love in an easy, organic manner. Deep breathing exercises can be helpful and many people report great results using the Emotional Freedom Technique, also known as EFT.

How do you feel about the health of your emotions, in particular the different types of love in your life? Keeping a weekly journal to record your feelings is a helpful way to stay aware of your emotional health. Start here by recording how you feel about your emotional health, and continue in the free space in the back of this book.

In what ways do you share your time with others, whether family and friends or a special nonprofit that inspires you? Make a list of potential nonprofit organizations you may be interested in helping.

Make a list of family members who may need your love.

How can you share your time with these family members? Record your experiences and how they made you feel on pages 65-67.

_____

_____

_____

_____

_____

_____

_____

_____

_____

_____

_____

_____

_____

_____

_____

_____

_____

_____

_____

_____

_____

Make a list of friends who may need your love.

How can you share your time with the friends you have listed? Record
your experiences and how they made you feel on pages 69-71.

Can you identify situations, people, or life experiences that helped you feel more loved, loving, and loveable? How often do you focus on those connections and experiences? Again, keep a journal of all the things you do, and can do, to support increasing love in your life. Use pages 72–75 to record specific interactions and how they made you feel.

What areas of your life diminish the love in your life? Make a list of the people, occupations, and other life experiences that decrease the feeling of love in your life. Are there ways to add love to any of these areas? How? And if not, what can you do to minimize your involvement with these people and situations? Use pages 76–79 to record specific interactions and how they made you feel.

Each morning when you rise, take five minutes to breathe slowly and calmly while focusing on your heart chakra in the same area where your physical heart is. How do you feel before versus after this short meditation? And over time, how does focusing on your heart chakra positively affect your life? Write it down in your special journal.

How much time do you spend cultivating unconditional love, such as caring for a pet or a child, or other altruistic activities? Caring for something or someone that can't reciprocate is a great way to develop unconditional love, as well as compassion. Try to make time each week to cultivate this type of love and journal about how it makes your heart feel.

VISHUDDHA— THE THROAT CHAKRA

THE FIFTH CHAKRA IS CALLED *VISHUDDHA*, WHICH means "purification." It's located in the throat and is blue in the Western chakra system. The Hindus originally described it as a whitish circular shape made up of sixteen purple and smoky gray petals. The gray comes from its association with the elephant Airavata, lord of all herbivorous animals. Within this circular shape is a blue triangle with a white circle. The circle references a full moon, and the moon can symbolize the invisible ether or etheric energy, itself connected to dreaming. Therefore, the throat chakra is also associated with dream yoga, or dreaming in general.

The major association of the throat chakra is with speech, communication, and creative expression. When the throat chakra is clear and open, we are able to let things go, especially our own past choices for good or ill, and express our views in a healthy way. We learn our lessons and move on; there's no dwelling on the past, present, or future anxieties, and we've gained wisdom from life experience. Our speech flows freely, we live in a state of healthy detachment, and this detachment makes it easier to experience powerful spirit dreams. The "ether" associated with the throat chakra is akin to our astral body, and at night it's believed that this etheric body leaves the body to dream.

On the other hand, when the throat chakra is blocked, the opposite is true. Our personal expression is limited, and we are wracked with guilt and shame over the past, fear the future, and find it difficult to live in the present moment. The roots of the word *Vishuddha* are "visha" and "shuddhi." Visha means "poison" and shuddhi means "purification." Therefore, when this chakra is closed, it is believed to become a poison in the body resulting in aging and death. When it's open and clear, it's seen as a purification agent that may contribute to exceptional longevity.

Resonance is this chakra's biggest influence. When our throat energy flows freely, we feel confident in who we are and easily share our voice with the world around us.

This chakra has a seed mantra sound associated with it, "Ham." It's pronounced "hahmm" rather than ham, like the pig. If you feel your throat chakra is blocked, repeating this mantra during meditation is believed to help purify it. Other means of clearing out the throat include headstands, such as yoga asanas like salamba sirsasana, the "king of asanas." Singing in general is also believed to be a healthy activity for the throat, whether in a dedicated kirtan active meditation or just singing along to your favorite song on the radio.

Let's look a bit deeper at a more esoteric side of the throat chakra called Dream Yoga. Dream Yoga is a very important part of Tibetan Buddhist practice, and it is seen as an important stepping stone on the path of transcendence from the endless cycles of birth and death. Many Eastern religions believe that we exist in an elaborate dream that only appears to be "real."

Working with dreams is believed to be an excellent way of realizing that our waking lives, too, are only dreams. This is accomplished by developing lucid dreaming, or waking up in a dream while the body remains asleep. Once lucid dreaming can be induced at will, it is possible to direct the course of dreams for spiritual benefit. The practices take years to master and are very elaborate, but Tibetan monks believe that mastering dreams prepares humans for the intense tidal wave of visual and sensory manifestations which occur just after death. Buddhist monks believe that we become entranced with these post-mortem manifestations and are drawn back into a new incarnation. However, if we can transcend these illusory, dreamlike images then we have a chance of breaking the endless cycle of death and rebirth.

In the throat chakra lies the beginnings of dream yoga practice. There are many visualizations, mantras, yogic, breathing, and other practices that rely on an active and healthy throat chakra for their successful completion. It's a fascinating aspect of Buddhism that is only now becoming more popular in the west.

The thyroid is the endocrine gland associated with the throat chakra. It's located in the throat, just below and to either side of the voice box. Thyroid hormones have many body regulation functions, mainly metabolism and body temperature during adulthood, but also have a great role in the healthy growth of the body during childhood development. Thyroid imbalance has unfortunately become all too common in the twenty-first century, especially for women.

Because of its location, the throat chakra has always been linked with hearing and the ears, and speech and the mouth. For the symbolic reasons mentioned previously, the throat chakra is also counterintuitively linked to dreaming and the etheric body. Another interesting throat chakra association is with overall quality of life. Vishuddha has poisonous and purifying aspects; it's indicated in the name itself. From the earliest Indian writings about vishuddha, it was believed that the state of health or dysfunction of the throat chakra was directly linked to the quality of one's life. A closed throat chakra can lead to the ruin of one's livelihood, whereas a healthy chakra supports qualities of leadership and success.

In the Western system, the throat chakra is mainly associated with clear communication and emotional expression. When the throat chakra is out of balance, there is stilted speech and emotional expression is dampened. Fear can be a major factor in both conditions and therefore facing fears is seen as a good way to open up the throat chakra.

Make a list of your fears. Be honest with yourself. Now, how do you feel looking at this list? Take a few moments and breathe into your heart from the heart chakra chapter, and allow feelings of love to embrace you as you go over your list of fears.

Over the next year choose one fear per month or week to work on. You don't have to do anything you're uncomfortable doing; simply reading about how other people faced a similar fear can have profoundly positive transformational effects on your throat chakra.

1. _____

_____

2. _____

_____

3. _____

_____

4. _____

_____

5. _____

_____

_____

_____

_____

6.

7.

8.

9.

10.

11.

12.

Are you able to express yourself freely? How easy is it for you to communicate thoughts and feelings to others?

_____

_____

_____

_____

_____

_____

_____

_____

_____

_____

_____

_____

_____

_____

_____

_____

_____

_____

_____

Are there people in your life with whom you wish you could communicate? What prevents you from doing so? Can you find creative ways to speak with them, whether it's in a letter, an email, or something else? What do you wish you could say to them?

Make a list of those people. Now find a private place where you won't be disturbed when speaking aloud and take the time to say out loud whatever it is you wish to say to them. Let it all out and then reflect.

How do you feel afterward? Do you still want to speak to them or is it enough to speak the words out loud?

_____

_____

_____

_____

_____

_____

_____

_____

_____

_____

_____

_____

_____

_____

_____

_____

_____

Do you remember your dreams? Keep a dream journal; it's not only fun but it trains your mind to pay attention to your dreams, an important step in the development of lucid dreaming.

AJNA—THE THIRD EYE CHAKRA

T HE NEXT CHAKRA IS CALLED *AJNA*, WHICH means "command." It is located between the brows, above the eyes, and near the top of the spine and has an indigo blue color in the modern Western system. In the traditional view, the Ajna chakra is white in color with two petals on either side. These petals symbolize a pair of nadis running up either side of the body that connect near the Ajna chakra. They are said to end at the nostrils.

The word *Ajna* means both self-command, achieved by overcoming the illusion of duality, and also the deep surrendering to the command or guidance of the guru. Ultimately, your own liberated self is the true guru, but until then, a guru is your selfless spiritual teacher.

When the Ajna chakra is activated, it is believed to coincide with a point in the spiritual development of a person where duality is overcome. So the Ajna chakra governs spiritual awakening. Its keyword is illumination. Attachment to the transient world around us fades and a unified mental state emerges. In the traditional Hindu view, when the third eye is awakened, it is possible to quickly burn through past karma, detach from the illusory sufferings of the world, and find true inner peace. Where an activated throat chakra indicates the achievement of a high level of self-purification, the third eye chakra's activation yields transcendence.

Psychic abilities, or siddhis, come alive with a fully activated third eye chakra. These are not mental powers, as the chakras do not correlate to the physical body. Rather, think of the chakras as pieces of a spiritual dynamo, that, when connected, bring about an energetic transformation of consciousness. In the process of spiritual awakening, the body is also transformed as a whole. Many people desire psychic ability and it is a completely natural phenomenon. Everyone is born with these abilities; it is only a matter of practice to activate them. When the Ajna chakra is spontaneously awakened, however, the psychic abilities can come all at once. The experience can be overwhelming, and in the traditional view in order to move past the third eye chakra and into the crown chakra, it is necessary to overcome all attachments to the siddhis. Psychic abilities can have a powerful effect on our life experience and letting go of what may feel like omniscient powers can be a difficult task.

Light is the third eye chakra's driving force, as both sunlight and the light of consciousness and illumination.

The third eye chakra is associated with the pineal and pituitary glands in contemporary Western systems. The pituitary is a "master" gland that regulates many hormonal functions in the body by sending signals to other glands in the body to produce hormones. Without the pituitary, the thyroid, adrenals, ovaries, and testes can malfunction. It's also responsible for releasing human growth hormone throughout our lives, regulating everything from overall growth to muscle and bone mass. The pituitary also regulates water balance and the production of milk in breastfeeding women.

The pineal gland controls sleep patterns and some sex hormones. In some more primitive species of animals, the pineal gland is a type of vestigial eye.

These glandular associations were not present in the earliest Tantric teachings but have developed over time. They are especially popular in contemporary Western systems. That's one of the most exciting things about working with chakras. Our understanding of what they are and how they function has progressed through the centuries as people from all over the world continue to investigate chakras. Whereas the Tantric system symbolically linked chakras with many different colors and shapes, various Sanskrit symbols, deities, and sounds, in the Western system the associations are more connected to parts of the body, rainbow colors, elements, sounds, astrological symbols, and even Kabballah mythology.

One way to activate the crown chakra is through meditation. Meditation over long periods of time helps us become more centered, less attached to the distractions of the world, and therefore puts us in a state of being more able to comprehend and transcend duality.

How often do you meditate? Do you feel more relaxed and centered afterward?

Are you in control of your life? If not, what are some areas that you wish you had more say in your life? When you feel out of control, what are some easy ways to be more self-directed, to experience the third eye chakra's concept of "self-command"?

_____

_____

_____

_____

_____

_____

_____

_____

_____

_____

_____

_____

_____

_____

_____

_____

_____

_____

Intuition and other psychic abilities are expressed by the activation of the third eye. Take time each week to cultivate your natural abilities; this will help stimulate the third eye chakra energy.

Start a journal and document the progression of your abilities. Starting with intuition is an easy one. Take time to learn common techniques to develop your natural psychic abilities.

A traditional way to help activate the third eye chakra is to repeat the mantra, "Ham," pronounced "hahmm," not ham. Spend a few minutes each week repeating this mantra while focusing on your third eye, located between your eyes.

7

SAHASRARA—
THE CROWN
CHAKRA

THE CROWN CHAKRA IS THE LAST AND SEVENTH energy center in most traditional chakra systems. Its Sanskrit name is *Sahasrara*, meaning "thousand-petalled," in reference to the infinite petals visualized with this chakra in the traditional system. Tibetan Buddhists imagine it with thirty-two petals, and it varies from tradition to tradition. In the Western system, it is seen as violet or white. The crown is located at the top of the head, in the place where our soft spot used to be when we were babies. Where the petals of the other chakras are typically drawn pointing up, the crown points down.

At its highest expression the crown chakra represents enlightenment, pure awareness, and an ability to escape from the endless cycles of birth and death from which most of us suffer. However, for us regular mortals it is also connected with inspiration and creativity, similar to the third eye chakra.

The consciousness of the crown chakra is beyond all duality, all grasping for temporal things like love, success, and so on. A person with an activated crown chakra can be described as glowing, literally. It's a state of consciousness wholly foreign to most of us, but to many Eastern traditions it represents the goal of the human experience and is believed to be possible to achieve in a single lifetime.

An out of balance crown chakra leads to insanity, the god complex of an unfortunately high number of contemporary gurus. Drugs are a huge hindrance to the development of chakras and the healthy expression of kundalini life-force energy, and part of this is because of the way drugs alter the human energy field. They can blow open the third eye chakra and allow the unprepared to experience psychic phenomenon in an unhealthy way, and they can also alter the expression of the crown chakra and make people feel like gods or goddesses when in reality they are anything but.

When properly activated, illumination is the key influential force of the crown chakra. Its essence connects us to the divine, to the entire cosmos. Or rather, its awakening allows us to remember the connections we've had all along to everything in existence.

There is no seed mantra associated with the crown chakra but the traditional sound is "Om." It is beyond all expression, and in a way represents the void between all things, the pause between the inhale and the exhale of creation. The moment between all things—that's how the crown chakra is connected to the All, through the in-between spaces between every manifested thing.

For each of the previous chakras there has been a corresponding part of the endocrine system to which most contemporary practitioners agree. However, this is not the case with the crown chakra. It has been linked to the entire endocrine system as well as specifically to the pineal and pituitary glands and to the hypothalamus region of the brain. The traditional yogic lore of Swami Ranganathananda (1908–2005) has a different idea about the crown chakra. He writes, "Yogis speak of a subtle nerve going to the crown of the head known as Susumna, which is located in the center of the spinal column. When the life energy of a Yogi, it is believed, passes through the susumna and goes through the aperture in the crown of the head, known as *brahma-randhra* or 'the opening leading to Brahma'—he will not be reborn in the world, but will steadily reach brahmaloka, the world of the cosmic Mind . . . the path thus traversed is known as the 'the northern path' or 'the path of light.'" This "subtle nerve" is part of the human energy field and is not connected to any particular gland in the body.

Students who work with the crown chakra need to be mindful of its instability in the beginning of a spiritual practice. It is possible to open the crown chakra too far but not yet know how to close it back down. This can lead to sensitivity to light and sound, headaches, and other physical symptoms. It is best to work with the crown chakra under the guidance of an experienced teacher to avoid these unpleasant experiences. Therefore, the following activity will help you connect to the spirit of the crown chakra indirectly, through active participation in service to humanity.

Reflecting on the qualities of the crown chakra, what are your goals on the spiritual path? Do you seek enlightenment or something less intense, perhaps some level of self-improvement but still wanting to enjoy the experience of being a human being? When embarking on the spiritual path it's helpful to write down your goals. Goals help keep everything in perspective and keep your journey as fun as possible.

The sacred word of the Crown chakra is Om or Aum. During your weekly meditations, if you find yourself reflecting on enlightenment repeat the word *om* over and over for several minutes, letting each word last as long as your exhalation. It is believed that creating sacred sounds has a positive effect on the body and soul, in this case the higher mind.

The crown chakra is associated with creativity. Make a list of your favorite creative activities and make the effort to be creative each week in some way. Have fun and express yourself!

The Crown chakra is also associated with that strange combination of complete detachment while cultivating intense unconditional love for all things. Detachment happens naturally on the spiritual path and is very different from what we experience as antisocial detachment in ordinary life. But unconditional love can be cultivated each and every day. In some small way each week commit an act of love without any hope of reward or recognition.

Lastly, reflect on the spiritual path of the unfolding chakras, from the root to the crown. How does it make you feel to imagine all your chakras open and healthy? Which chakras do you feel are the most open and flowing and which ones need some attention?

Working with the chakras is a great metaphor for life. As you work on your life issues and face your fears, open yourself to new experiences and regain a sense of wonder toward our mysterious world by working on your chakras, your everyday life may also improve in profound and personal ways. Enjoy your unique spiritual journey as you explore the chakras. Use the following pages to reflect on your journey working with the major seven chakras.

ACKNOWLEDGMENTS

Thank you to the incredible team at Sterling. Deep gratitude to Kate Zimmermann for bringing this beautiful journal into being. Thank you so much to the talented designers, Elizabeth Lindy and Sharon Jacobs, who made this book so gorgeous. The sales, distribution, and marketing teams at Sterling are the best in the business. We are extraordinarily grateful to have our books and journals in so many stores!

Amy is filled with gratitude to have Krystin White, Ashley Moreno, and Sarah Hall at Sarah Hall Productions getting the word out about her books.

The woman who makes it all possible is our marvelous agent, Lisa Hagan. We feel so lucky to have her in our corner that we dedicated this book to her!

ABOUT THE AUTHORS

AMY LEIGH MERCREE is a bestselling author, holistic health expert, and medical intuitive. She speaks and teaches internationally, sharing Next Level Healing, Meet Your Guides, Mindfulness Meditation, and Bestseller Bootcamp classes.

Amy is the author of *The Spiritual Girl's Guide to Dating*, *A Little Bit of Chakras*, *Joyful Living: 101 Ways to Transform Your Spirit and Revitalize Your Life*, *The Chakras and Crystals Cookbook*, *The Compassion Revolution: 30 Days of Living from the Heart*, *A Little Bit of Meditation*, *Essential Oils Handbook*, *Apple Cider Vinegar Handbook*, *A Little Bit of Mindfulness*, *The Mood Book: Crystals, Oils, and Rituals to Elevate Your Spirit*, *A Little Bit of Goddess: An Introduction to the Divine Feminine*, two other *Little Bit of Journals*, and the *100 Days to Calm Journal*.

She has been featured in *Glamour Magazine*, *Women's Health*, *Inc. Magazine*, *Shape*, *The Huffington Post*, *Your Tango*, *Mind Body Green*, *CBS*, *NBC*, *FOX*, *Hello Giggles*, *Reader's Digest*, *The Oprah Magazine*, *Forbes*, *First for Women*, *Country Living*, *Bustle*, *Elite Daily*, *Thrive Global*, *Poosh*, and many more.

Amy is fast becoming one of the most quoted women on the web. See what all the buzz is about @AmyLeighMercree on social.

CHAD MERCREE is a bestselling author and personal development expert. He has written books on spirituality since 2012 including *A Little Bit of Buddha*, *The Way of the Psychic Heart*, and *A Little Bit of Chakras*.

Chad's work has been featured in *Spirituality & Health Magazine*, *Aspire Magazine*, and *Truth Be Told Radio*, to name a few. His passions are personal development, the natural world, and ancient history. You can learn more about him and get personal development and spiritual healing hints and tips at www.chadmercree.com.

To download your FREE Chakra Toolkit and power up
all of your chakras right now go to
www.amyleighmercree.com/chakratoolkit using the
password **CHAKRAS.**